Ox
Herding
at
Morgan's Bay

by Master Sheng-yen

Edited by Mark Baldwin &
Christopher Marano

Editors: Mark Baldwin
                Christopher Marano

Translator: Paul Kennedy

Illustrations: Ling-yun Shih

Cover and
Book Design: Trish Ing

Photographer: Mark Baldwin

Dharma Drum Publications is the publishing activity of

The Institute of Chung-Hwa Buddhist Culture
90-56 Corona Avenue
Elmhurst, New York 11373

Library of Congress Catalog Card Number 88-51571
ISBN 0-9609854-3-3

Acknowledgement

We would like to acknowledge and thank Ling-yun Shih for her fine, original renditions of the *Ten Ox Herding Pictures.*

Ling-yun Shih, an artist and calligrapher, has drawn many of the covers and inside illustrations for the Ch'an Magazine, one of our center's publications. Her drawings for *Ox Herding at Morgan's Bay* are simple & spare, yet they convey the spirit of the traditional pictures.

Since Master Sheng-yen has offered a 20th century commentary on the Ox Herding analogy, we felt it would be appropriate to have a 20th century inter-pretation of the drawings as well. We hope that Master Sheng-yen's words and Ling-yun Shih's images are as timeless as the *Ten Ox Herding Pictures.*

Contents

Preface

In the spring of 1987, I held a retreat at Morgan's Bay, a Zen community in Surry, Maine. For four evenings I talked about the path of Zen, or Ch'an, practice, using the *Ten Ox Herding Pictures* as a model. My talks were informal and spontaneous, geared primarily to help the retreat participants overcome obstacles they faced in their practice. Four evenings is not a long time to spend discussing such an important work, but the participants told me that they found the talks to be valuable. They wished for the lectures to be transcribed and edited, and since they offered to do it, I gladly agreed.

The ox herding pictures provide an analogy to help explain the process of Ch'an practice. The ever-watchful, ever-patient ox herder is a model for Ch'an practitioners, who should constantly watch their minds of vexation, and who should not be influenced by the external environment.

Many versions of the ox herding pictures exist. During the T'ang dynasty (618-906), Master Pai-chang used the ox herding analogy, and later, Master Nan-ch'uan P'u-yuan and Shih-kung Hui-tsan, who were disciples of Master Ma-tzu, used similar analogies with buffaloes in place of oxen. The most popular version, however, is attributed to K'uo-an Shih-yuan, who was a Lin-chi (Rinzai) master during the Sung Dynasty

(960-1279). His version can be found in chapters forty-six and forty-seven of the *Extended Arguments*. The ox herding analogy is also found in volume two of the sastra of the *Great Wisdom of the Paramitas*. Furthermore, in the *Bequeathed Teachings of the Buddha*, there is a saying that one should not be lax in one's effort. One should be like the person who herds an ox: always vigilant.

Other versions of the ox herding pictures exist. There is a version with five pictures, another with six, still another with eight. I will use the most common and popular version – Master K'uo-an Shih-yuan's *Ten Ox Herding Pictures*. In the original version, four lines of verse accompany each of the ten pictures. I will not discuss the meaning of the words. Instead, I will comment directly on the meaning of the pictures.

The numerous versions of the ox herding pictures are highly regarded by practitioners in China and Japan, and more recently, in the West. Renditions in English can be found in *Zen Flesh, Zen Bones*, transcribed by Nyogen Senzaki and Paul Reps, and in *The Three Pillars of Zen*, compiled and edited by Roshi Philip Kapleau. Two versions appear in D.T. Suzuki's *Manual of Zen Buddhism*. In the latter version, which is by an unknown author, the ox gradually whitens until it completely disappears, ending with a blank circle. There is also a book on the teachings of Zen master Dogen, in which the author, Francis Dojun Cook, adopts the analogy for his book's title: *How to Raise an Ox*.

The ox herding pictures are profound in meaning and wisdom, so one needn't worry that there are too many commentaries. Perhaps my approach is somewhat different from those of others. Whether it is or isn't does not matter. I hope only that this commentary is of value to readers and practitioners.

Morgan's Bay

April 13 - 16, 1987

Introduction

This version of the *Ten Ox Herding Pictures*, which illustrates the different states of mind at different levels of practice, was created by a Ch'an master during the Sung dynasty, but the idea of looking for the ox dates back to the T'ang dynasty.

At that time there was a monk who was in charge of stoking fires for the cooking pots down below the kitchen of a monastery. One day a famous Ch'an master observed him at his work and asked, "What are you doing?"

The monk said, "I'm watching the ox."

The master asked him, "In what way are you watching the ox?"

The monk replied, "Every time the ox tries to wander off to eat grass, I rein it in and put it back to work." In other words, every time his mind wandered, the monk pulled it back to the job or method.

It's normal for an ox to eat grass sometimes. In fact, it's necessary for survival. But in this story, the ox is eating grass when it should be working. The ox herder yokes the ox with a rope and stick; practitioners yoke their wandering minds with methods of practice.

Training an ox requires great patience. If your ox wanders off to eat grass, what should you do? Should you kill it? No, you patiently pull it back to its work, as often as necessary. You should never get upset with yourself if your mind wanders off the method, or if you're not practicing properly. Just catch yourself, and be aware of the digression. This very awareness is proper practice. This is watching the ox. Training the mind is like training a wild ox, only harder.

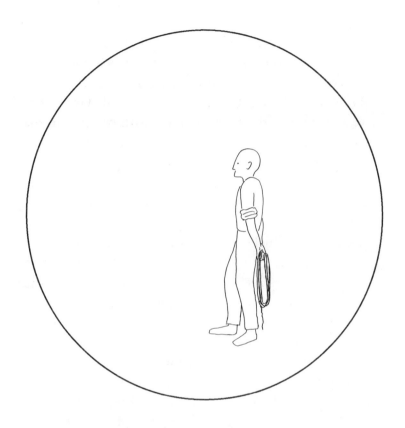

The First Picture

The first picture is called "looking for the ox." The ox herder walks with a rope, which is a leash for the ox, but the ox is nowhere to be found. The ox is his most valuable possession, so the ox herder searches diligently.

In the early stages of practice, a person has heard that within him is the Buddha mind – pure nature –

but he has never seen it. Having faith that the pure nature exists, however, the person strives to find it.

Throughout the pictures, the ox herder represents the mind or thought in the process of cultivation. The ox, however, varies in accordance with changes in the states of mind. In the early pictures, the ox is wild and represents the mind that needs training. As the mind becomes clearer and more stable, the ox becomes tamer. Later pictures relate to the stage of practice when Buddha nature, or self-nature, has been revealed. Eventually, the ox disappears altogether.

Are you searching for the ox? Why have you come on a Ch'an retreat? Why shut yourself off from the rest of the world for several days, submitting to rules and regulations, sitting through pain, forfeiting everyday indulgences and comforts, and seemingly gaining nothing for your efforts? Not many people would be willing to put themselves through such hardship in order to see their own nature.

Either you are partially convinced that there is such a thing as seeing into one's own nature, and are willing to give intense practice a try, or you are thoroughly convinced, and you're willing to accept any hardships you may encounter.

Do you believe that if you practice Ch'an you will one day achieve enlightenment, or see into your true nature? What will you do if you do not succeed? If you practice until your dying day and haven't attained enlightenment, how will you feel? Will you think all your effort has been in vain. Think about it.

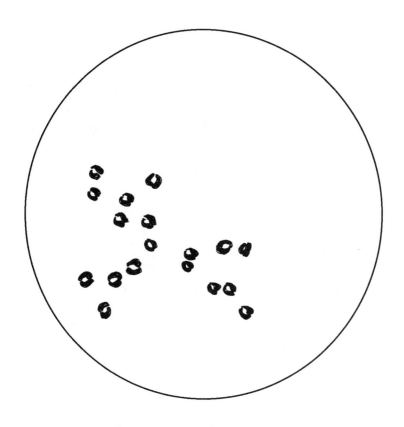

The Second Picture

In the second picture, the ox herder sees the tracks of the ox. The ox herder has not seen or found the ox, but he has discovered tracks — some going eastward, some westward, others going in many directions and then stopping suddenly. The ox (mind) is still undisciplined, and has a wandering, erratic nature. Seeing the tracks increases the ox herder's confidence that the ox exists, and that it can be found.

The second picture describes the person who has come in contact with an enlightened master, or who has read about enlightenment in Buddhist sutras or lectures. He believes more strongly that Buddha nature is real, and that Sakyamuni Buddha and the great patriarchs existed. He realizes that those who attained enlightenment in the past were ordinary people like himself, and so he believes that he can attain enlightenment too. He begins to practice with greater faith and diligence.

At this level, sometimes efforts are rewarded and sometimes they are not. At times a person will feel confident: "Yes, I can achieve enlightenment." Other times he or she will feel despondent: "I'm not a good practitioner. I'm dull and slow, and I don't have a lot of potential."

The person's practice will be erratic. Sometimes he'll practice hard, and other times he'll grow lax and drop the practice. But there are people who will always be firm in their determination to practice. What kind of person are you?

Student: Shih-fu, you speak about enlightenment, but today in America there are people handing out little diplomas saying, "If you follow my teaching, you'll get enlightened." The word enlightenment seems to have lost its meaning.

Shih-fu: I have always said we should emphasize the process, not the final result. In fact, the process itself is the final result.

Enlightenment is discussed in books, but it does seem to be unclear exactly what constitutes enlightenment, and how difficult it is to achieve it. Some books or people make it seem like it is a simple thing to accomplish. Whether enlightenment is easy or difficult to achieve depends on the practitioner.

One discourse in the Buddhist texts describes sixteen different types of enlightenment. There are experiences where one has not actually seen the true nature. There are experiences where one does see the true nature, but the experience recedes. And then there is great enlightenment, which is complete and permanent.

Many of these so-called enlightenment experiences are physiological and psychological responses which rise in the body and mind as a result of practice. Some people feel a sense of joy, or feel that the body and mind have been liberated. Are these true enlightenment experiences? No, not according to Ch'an. They are just feelings, emotional states. However, they are valuable experiences. It's permissible to call these enlightenment experiences, because during such times the person's mind is different than it usually is. The mind is brighter, and for a while the person may have no vexation. But after a few days, hours, or even minutes, the person will encounter something that gives rise to greed or aversion, and again vexations will appear.

There are many people who, when they refer to Ch'an enlightenment, are actually referring to these sort of experiences. However, if such a person were to ask for affirmation from a capable Ch'an master, the master would probably scold him rather than acknowledge the experience. Acknowledging false enlightenments does more harm than good.

True enlightenment is seeing into your self-nature, and achieving a mind of equanimity. The nature of the mind of equanimity is empty. Emptiness means that the mind does not exist, so if a person thinks he has been enlightened, yet he feels elated, or believes he has accomplished something great, then he's hasn't seen his self-nature.

The best attitude is to understand and accept that it is the process of practice which is important, not the end result. As the ox herding pictures illustrate, the main objective is seeing into your self-nature. But, even after seeing your self-nature, there is still a lot of work to be done. Remember, in this picture, the ox herder has only seen tracks, and not the ox itself. Do not mistake the tracks for the ox.

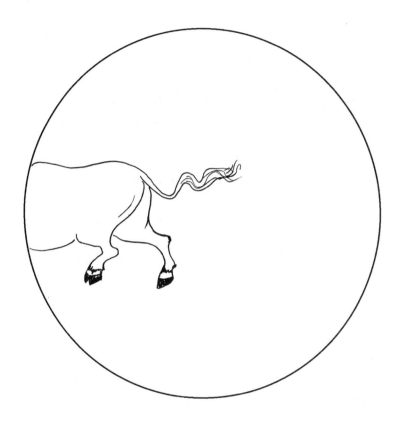

The Third Picture

After looking for a long time, the ox herder sees the
tail of the ox sticking out from behind a tree. He's very
happy, but the ox is still not in his hands.

This is equivalent to seeing your self-nature for the
first time. It is comparable to traveling a long distance
and finally spotting a high mountain (your goal) in the
distance – close enough to see, but too far away to

climb. How high it really is and what is on it is still not clear. Also, you lose sight of the mountain when the skies are cloudy. But at least you have seen the mountain, or in the case of the pictures, the ox. Faith is firmly established.

In Ch'an, this stage is sometimes called "having opened one eye." But there are many eyes – physical eyes, Dharma eyes, wisdom eyes, liberation eyes, and others – so you are still nearly blind. With this type of experience, you might also say that your eye opened for a moment, and then closed again.

Imagine walking on a dark night, when it's raining hard and pitch black. Suddenly, a bolt of lightning flashes and illuminates the area for a brief moment. Before, you wandered and stumbled in the darkness, but now, because of the lightning flash, you are aware of your immediate surroundings. You can walk with certainty, but only for a short distance. Up ahead it's still dark.

No matter how you describe it, this type of experience is valuable, even it isn't deep. Are there people who open all their eyes and don't close them again? Yes, there are. But such people are rare. What is it that I'm talking about?

Student: It sounds like what Zen masters call *kensho*.

Shih-fu: Is *kensho* a big deal?

Student: From what I've observed, no.

Shih-fu: Is a person who has seen his self-nature a common person, or is he a saintly person or sage?

Student: During the time the eye remains open, which may be a day or a week or a month, he would be a sage. But after it closes, he would be a common person again.

Shih-fu: Actually, the person who has had that experience is the same as a common person. He still has the same vexations. At least now, however, he'll be more aware of vexations as they arise.

These questions address situations which can be dangerous. For instance, a person who has had this experience may believe that he no longer has any vexations, and that he is truly liberated. When vexations do appear, he'll then doubt that the experience was really of any value. It's also possible that, even after vexations reappear, the person may deceive himself and others by acting like a saintly person.

There are three ways for a teacher to help a person like this. One way is to let the person know that although his *kensho* is good, it is still shallow. It is like a baby bird who knows enough to open its mouth to eat, but who has yet to grow feathers. How can it think of flying at this point?

A person who has a shallow *kensho* experience and thinks he's qualified to be a master is endangering himself and others. It must be made clear to the person that he has to continue working hard in his practice. He is still featherless.

The second way for a master to help this person is to remind him of the five main precepts of Buddhism: no killing, no stealing, no sexual misconduct, no false speech (lying, talking behind people's backs, or falsely claiming you are a master), and not indulging in intoxicants.

A deeply enlightened master need not pay attention to the precepts, because his wisdom and *samadhi* power are never apart from the precepts. There is no need to add any rules. For the person who has just had a *kensho* experience, however, the precepts are like the nest which protects the baby bird, and it would be as dangerous for the person to leave the precepts as it would for the bird to leave the nest.

There are practices which seem to contradict this. Have you heard about certain Buddhists groups where monks drink alcohol, calling it "wisdom soup?"

Student: I've heard of something like that. The word is *upaya*. It means that expedient methods, which can include acts of misbehavior, are justifiable if it is done for the good of the student. As I understand it, the idea is to break the narrow conception of the student. One master, for example, would eat hamburgers in front of his students if they became too attached to the idea of not eating meat.

Shih-fu: It is true that great masters can use expedient methods to help students. For example,

Ch'an master Nan-ch'uan cut a cat in half as a means of teaching his disciples. But when lesser masters try to imitate great Ch'an masters, it usually leads to problems. I consider myself to be a lesser Ch'an master, so I'm not going to imitate the great ones. In the history of Ch'an and Zen Buddhism, only one great master out of many killed a cat. Generally speaking, Ch'an masters should maintain the precepts. Master Hsu-yun, probably the greatest Ch'an master in recent history, strictly adhered to the precepts.

The third way to deal with a recent *kensho* experience is to adhere to the outer forms and rituals of the practice. Having definite forms of practice, attire and behavior helps to create a better environment in which to practice. Of course, I'm referring to monks and nuns, but the same holds true for lay practitioners. Maintaining the proper outer form, the proper demeanor, will help a practitioner not to stray from the practice.

Actually, if a person who has had a shallow enlightenment continues to practice hard, adheres to the precepts, and maintains the rituals, then to a certain extent he is in a position to help other people.

I am sorry to say that Chinese practitioners do not keep up this outer form. Today it seems most practitioners are sloppy in their practice. For this reason you don't see many Chinese Ch'an masters. There are more Japanese Zen masters. In the future, I will try to train students and disciples in this aspect of the practice.

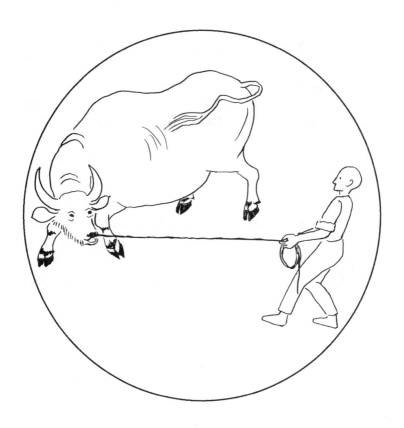

The Fourth Picture

In this picture, the ox herder has caught the ox and has gotten the rope around it, but it is still wild and resistant. The ox wants to wander in the fields and eat grass.

This picture refers to the person who has continued to practice diligently after seeing his self-nature. He now has two eyes open, and they won't close again. His eyes may get heavy at times and not see things clearly, but they are always ready to open wide again.

At this stage the person has control of his vexations. Vexations may still rise in the mind, but they are controlled in body and speech. Although thoughts of hate might emerge, the person could not be driven to harm someone, whereas an ordinary person still has the potential to harm others. There might be thoughts of lust, but they would not carry over into words and actions. Such a person truly maintains the precepts.

Is someone at this stage qualified to be a teacher? If there is a master around who is more advanced, the person should continue to study with him. However, if there are no other masters, the person should try to help those who have not yet reached his level.

Where do you stand in these pictures? Where is your ox? Seeing your self-nature is not an easy thing to do, is it?

The Fifth Picture

The fifth picture is the true ox herding picture. The ox herder, with a whip in one hand and a rein through the ox's nose, is leading the animal. The ox can now be considered tame, though it may wander off if the ox herder becomes lax and doesn't pay attention.

Self-cultivation now comes naturally; it is part of one's everyday life. But a few vexations may remain, so one must continue working on *samadhi* in order to control them.

Ch'an enlightenment, which can be achieved through *kung-an* (*koan*) practice, is not gained through *samadhi* or concentration power. *Kung-an* practice and *samadhi* practice are different types of concentration.

Think of *kung-an* practice as a method of taking one's vexation, or wandering thoughts, and pushing them all into one concentrated spot until there is no place to push them any more, at which point they explode, just as a balloon bursts when it is over-inflated. We use "doubt sensation" to concentrate the mind, to focus it until the final explosion. The strength of the explosion depends on the force behind it. The balloon may burst into many pieces, or only get a small hole in it. In *kung-an* practice, the goal is to thoroughly blow apart the concentrated mind.

I also use the analogy of throwing a rock into water. If a person with little vexation uses the "doubt" method, it is like throwing a big rock into a small puddle. The water is scattered, and all that remains is the rock. That's the aim of the method. However, if the person practicing has many vexations and doesn't really penetrate the method, then the final result will be like throwing a pebble into a lake. There'll be a splash, but not enough to see the bottom of the lake.

Focusing on the doubt sensation is not the same as *samadhi,* which is a deeper, more unmoving concentration. *Samadhi* can help to keep the mind peaceful and stable, with minimal emotions.

Samadhi practice is necessary after a *kensho* experience. With this practice you can gain full control of suppressed vexations, and disperse vexations which have already manifested. However, the *samadhi* you cultivate after a *kensho* experience is quite different from the *samadhi* you practice before having seen your self-nature.

Therefore, the person who has seen his self-nature still needs both precepts and *samadhi*. The precepts will help prevent the person from doing things that will cause more vexation, and *samadhi* will help to eliminate those vexations which have not yet manifested.

The Sixth Picture

The sixth picture is called "riding the ox back home." When we talked about seeing the self-nature for the first time, I used an analogy of spotting a mountain in the distance, but not knowing how far away it was. The mountain refers to our original home — Buddhahood.

While the *kensho* experience is seeing one's Buddha nature, it is not the same as becoming a buddha. But in riding the ox, one is on the path back home.

In the picture, the ox herder is playing a flute. The ox still has a ring through its nose, but there's no need to hang onto the rein, which is thrown around the ox's horn. The ox herder doesn't bother directing the ox, because it is familiar with the way. Here, practice is effortless. The person's six sense organs are purified. That is to say, when he comes into contact with things in the environment, vexations do not rise. The person is aware of the environment, but the environment does not generate feelings of greed or anger in him.

Someone at this level feels close to all that he sees, hears, or feels. It's as if the whole world is a Buddha world. Everything is proclaiming the Dharma. The person knows that practice is still necessary. He knows there is a mind that needs cultivation, so he continues to practice. Practice, however, is effortless.

There is no need to encourage the person to practice. Nothing can come between him and practice along the path. In fact, everything he does is practice. When a person reaches this stage, he is safe. Precepts, *samadhi* and wisdom become part of his being. The person no longer thinks or says, "I need to practice."

When a person reaches this level, could he do something which is normally considered evil or wrong, and still not be breaking the precepts? For practitioners, it is best to respect and maintain the precepts. In regard to the question I asked, the answer is clear. If *samadhi* and precepts are one with a person at this level, then he cannot break the precepts. Anyone who commits an unwholesome act would not be at the level of the person in the sixth picture.

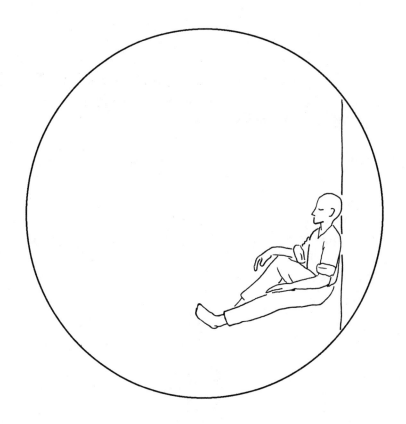

The Seventh Picture

In the seventh ox herding picture we see only the ox herder.

The ox is off sleeping, but where it is sleeping is not our concern. It is quite different from the beginning stages where we could not find the ox.

Beginning practice is like swimming upstream. A practitioner must work hard to stay afloat and make headway against the current. Great effort is required. But at the stage of the seventh picture, the swimmer is gone. He has become one with the water, and water is all there is to be found. Is there still swimming, then? At this point, there's nothing to do.

In the sixth picture, practice (self-cultivation) is effortless, yet self-cultivation continues. At the seventh stage, self-cultivation ceases, but the person is still there.

In the *Platform Sutra*, the Sixth Patriarch, Hui-neng, says that such a person no longer has love, hate, or aversion in his mind. He can stretch out his legs from the lotus position and lie down. There is no more need to sit.

There's a story about a monk who lived during the Ming dynasty. He was enlightened, but he didn't have a temple of his own or anywhere to stay, so he just wandered around. One day he came across a monastery with statues of heavenly kings in front, and he fell asleep right under the feet of one of the statues. He was snoring loudly when a high government official rode by. The official heard the snoring and became angry. He said, "Who's this? What kind of monk lies around and doesn't get up when I come?"

The monk heard him and said, "It's only me, a monk with nothing to do."

The official raged, "What! A monk with nothing to do! How can you have nothing to do? You have meditation. You can recite the sutras. You can prostrate. How can you say a monk has nothing to do?"

The monk said, "I don't have to do any of that."

After a while, the government official understood that he was not an ordinary monk. He reached the seventh stage of the ox herding pictures. But on this retreat we have a lot to do. We're not up to the seventh stage of the ox herding pictures, so we must continue to meditate.

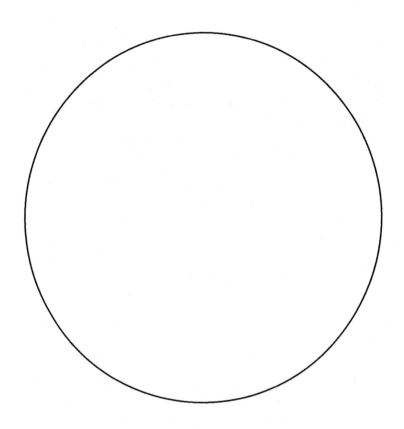

The Eighth Picture

In the eighth picture there is neither an ox nor a person. There is only a circle, the frame of a picture. At this stage, the ox represents Buddha nature, or self-nature, and the man represents the mind or the thought that is cultivating.

If there is one, then it follows that there are two. There can never be one; there can never be only a subject, only an object. A subject cannot exist without an object. All things exist in relationship to something else. If there's an ox, then there is a person, and if there is a person, then there is an ox. Neither are in the eighth picture, neither exist. One is the subject, the other is the object. They must exist together. They cannot be without each other.

Who experiences this self-nature? It can only be experienced by someone who has left behind his self. If there is still self-nature to be experienced, that is not true self-nature. Self-nature is explained only to those people who haven't experienced it. For the person who has experienced it, there really is nothing to speak of.

Let's return to the analogy of the swimmer. When the swimmer is separate from the water, the water exists for him. But when he becomes one with the water, when he is the water, does the water exist for him? If he is the water, can the water have an existence of its own?

If "you" are "it", is this one or two? On the surface it looks like one, because you are it, and it is it. There is only one "it." But how can you know that there is "one" unless there's a second entity observing it. As I said before, if there's one, then there is definitely two.

"Before enlightenment" and "after enlightenment" are different. Before enlightenment you only know about self-nature. After enlightenment, you are self-nature. When you arrive at the mountain, you become one with the mountain. Is there still a mountain to return to? No. At that point you don't know where the mountain is. Why? Because you are it.

Maybe you think you can grab hold of yourself — you can grab your nose and say, "This is myself." But if it were truly yourself, you wouldn't be able to grab hold of it. It wouldn't be separate from yourself, something other than yourself.

When you become one with self-nature there no longer is self-nature. There is no person who is cultivating and no cultivating that needs to be done. Since there is not one, of course there are not two. At this point, do you exist or not?

If there is a consciousness, then there are definitely two, because consciousness only manifests when it comes in contact with something else. There has to be relativity in order for consciousness to exist. There is no absolute consciousness.

There are no words to describe this experience, and there is no way to experience it with the mind. You cannot communicate it to others. If you use words to express it, then you're already dealing with it relatively. It is also the same if you try to express it with the mind or with thoughts. At the eighth stage, there is no big and no small, no near and no far.

Even absoluteness is relative. Great unity, supreme absoluteness, all things like this are relative terms. If there is something that is absolute, then there must be something that is not absolute. If you experience a state of great unity, then you are at the level of "great self," not at the level of "no self."

In other religions and philosophies, you do not find a solution to this puzzle – only in Buddhism: Nothingness is true existence.

Although the circle in this picture is empty, it would be better if there were no circle at all. Making the circle implies that something is still there – a great unity. In Ch'an there are instances where a disciple asks a question, and a Ch'an master makes a form of a circle, and then erases it. In doing so the master emphasizes that there is no absoluteness. If you have a circle, then attachment still exists, and that is not true enlightenment.

In the seventh picture, there is nothing left for the person to do. Now, in the eighth picture, not only is there nothing for the ox herder to do, there isn't even an ox herder.

One could say that such a person has reached the highest level attainable in terms of eliminating vexations and achieving wisdom. In terms of wisdom, this stage and the stage of Buddhahood are the same.

The Ch'an sect often speaks of two types of wisdom. One is "root wisdom," or "fundamental wisdom," which eliminates the source of all personal vexations. At the same time, the Buddha has another kind of wisdom, called "acquired wisdom," which is wisdom that is used to help sentient beings.

When a person reaches the stage of the eighth picture, he doesn't actually disappear from daily life. He does have an effect on things that occur around him. It is not like snow that has melted away, or water that has turned to steam. If it were, it would not be the way of Buddhism. That line of reasoning would come under the heading of nihilism.

There are people who experience emptiness, and then adopt a negative attitude towards things, shying away from daily life, even thinking, "The sooner I die the better." Such a mentality would definitely be a step off the Buddha path. I've seen quite a few people act this way.

One woman didn't want to go back to her family or have anything to do with her husband. That is wrong. Another person was a chairman of the board of a company. He was ready to quit his position and give up everything, including his family. Sometimes people become suicidal. These people have serious problems. Such an experience of emptiness is especially dangerous for people with mental or emotional instability.

The eighth picture is not to be confused with nihilism. Also, at the eighth stage, the person enters directly into the stage depicted by the ninth picture.

The Ninth Picture

The ninth picture is entitled "returning to the origin."
At this stage, the person returns to the world, and
everything is perceived just as it is by ordinary people.

There is a famous Ch'an saying stating that in the
beginning, before one practices, mountains are mountains and rivers are rivers. Then as one penetrates the
practice, at a certain point, mountains are no longer

mountains and rivers are no longer rivers. In the end, mountains are again mountains and rivers are again rivers. The ninth picture describes the stage where mountains are again mountains and rivers are again rivers.

The mountains and rivers that were perceived before one started the practice and those that are perceived now are the same, with one very important difference. Before enlightenment they were perceived with a mind of discrimination and attachment. Now there is no attachment. At this level, all things can be used to help sentient beings on the path to enlightenment.

There was a disciple, Yan-shan, who asked Master Wei-shan, "If myriad phenomena suddenly appeared before you, what would you do?"

The master replied, "Green is not yellow, long is not short. Each dharma abides in its own place. It has nothing to do with me." That is to say, phenomena are perceived, but they have no relation to an enlightened being. However, if this is not fully understood, it can cause problems. Some people go astray and do things which are not correct. They see everything as being the same, but it is not that way. Other people's wives and husbands are still other people's wives and husbands, other people's money is still other people's money. Wordly conventions are still valid. We should not disregard them. In the ninth stage, all phenomena are just as they are. We don't treat them in a haphazard, reckless manner.

Sometimes, Ch'an masters disorder phenomena while interacting with students by saying or doing contradictory things, but it always involves practice. If I went around in my daily life and said, "Bananas grow underground and ginger grows on trees, fish fly in the sky and sheep graze under water," people would think I've just been released from a mental institution. The person at the ninth stage honors worldly conventions.

Student: What about the story of the master who burned the statue of the Buddha? Didn't he break important conventions?

Shih-fu: He only did that once, before he was a master. He did it to express a truth of the Dharma to his master in order to gain certification that he was enlightened. He would not frivolously chop up the Buddha statue and use it for firewood.

There is another story in a similar vein about a monk who was going along with a heavy wheelbarrow full of mud. The master, sitting beside the road, stuck his leg out in front of the wheelbarrow. The disciple stopped and said, "Would you please move your leg? I must pass"

The master said, "This here? This isn't a leg."

So the disciple said, "Okay then, I'll keep going," and he rolled over the leg and broke it.

Again, this is not an ordinary story, and it is only a single occurence. Throughout all of Ch'an and Zen history it only happened once. Disciples don't break their masters' legs. These actions are all performed to certify that, at that moment, the realm which the person is in is not the everyday realm. It's not the ninth stage, either. It's closer to the seventh or eighth stage.

The Tenth Picture

In the tenth picture, the enlightened person is returning to save sentient beings. One hand is outstretched to all sentient beings, and in the other hand is a bag with all sorts of things, which he distributes according to need.

At any time and any place, the enlightened person is prepared to help other sentient beings to attain enlightenment. There's no definite form that the person takes. The person may be a Ch'an master, or a lay person, or even someone who is looked down upon by others.

The tenth picture shows that the person can manifest in any form, take on any personality or walk of life, and help sentient beings. But no matter how the person manifests, he always follows the conventions of that form. If he takes the form of a monk, he portrays a monk maintaining the precepts. If he manifests as a lay person, then he follows the conventions of that form.

This person is somewhat different from the normal Ch'an or Zen master, who is only able to help certain individuals. When an enlightened being of the tenth stage takes a particular form to help sentient beings, he'll be limited, according to the form he has taken, as to which sentient beings he can help. But he can reappear later, or in another life, in a different form, to help other sentient beings.

In Taiwan there was a woman who claimed that she was saved, so to speak, by her daughter. Being saved can mean being enlightened, but in this case it meant that the woman was introduced to Buddhism and the practice. I asked how old the daughter was, and she said, "Eight years old."

I thought, "This must be a very special daughter," and so I went to see her. She seemed to be a normal little girl.

I asked the woman, "Why do you think your daughter saved you?"

The woman replied, "Since my daughter was born, various things that have happened to her have steered me to Buddhism. Therefore, I say my daughter is a bodhisattva who has saved me."

What do you think? Is the daughter a bodhisattva? As far as the mother is concerned, she is. Perhaps, though, she is an enlightened being at the tenth stage who has taken the form of the daughter in this life.

Have you come in contact with any bodhisattvas or Ch'an masters like this? If not, how come you're here studying Ch'an? We should look upon anybody who helps us in the practice or who leads us to the path as being a tenth stage enlightened person.

A disciple asked Master Nan-ch'uan (the one who cut the cat in half), "Where are you going after you die?"

He said, "I'm going to the foot of the hill to be reborn as a cow."

The disciple looked puzzled and said, "If you're going to become a cow, then what am I going to become?"

The master said, "You can become a cow too, but if you do, it will be for the sake of eating grass."

Nothing was said after that. It's up to you to figure out what Master Nan-ch'uan meant.

About the Author

Master Sheng-yen has received transmission in the two major branches of Ch'an (Zen) Buddhism: the Lin-chi (Rinzai) and Ts'ao-tung (Soto) schools. Born on a farm outside Shanghai, he left home at thirteen to become a monk. As a young man during the period of communist unrest, he went to southern Taiwan, where he spent six years in the mountains in solitary retreat. Later, he continued to study Buddhism in Japan, receiving a doctorate degree in Buddhist Literature from Rissho University in Tokyo. Master Sheng-yen is the Dharma heir of Master Tung-chu and Master Ling-yuan, both of whom also emigrated from China to Taiwan. He is a second-generation descendant of the patriarch of modern Ch'an Buddhism, Master Hsu-yun.

Master Sheng-yen has written over thirty books on Buddhism and Ch'an in Chinese, English and Japanese. He divides his time between the United States and Taiwan.